The Search for

Inner Peace

Other published and upcoming titles from
Islamic Audiobooks Central

Did God Become Man?

The True Message of Jesus Christ

The Best Way to Live and Die

Muhammad's Prophethood: An Analytical View

The Best Way to Live and Die

The Global Messenger

Clear Your Doubts About Islam

The Search for

Inner Peace

BILAL PHILIPS

ISLAMIC
AUDIOBOOKS CENTRAL

ISBN:

978-0-473-52219-3 (Paperback)

978-0-473-52221-6 (Kindle)

978-1-094-21736-9 (Audiobook)

A catalogue record for this book is available from the
National Library of New Zealand

Also available as an audiobook from

ISLAMIC
AUDIOBOOKS CENTRAL

Islamic Audiobooks Central

https://islamicaudiobookscentral.com

CONTENTS

I

The topic of inner peace addresses a universal need. There is nobody on this planet that does not desire inner peace. It is not a desire that is new to our time; rather, it is something that everybody has been searching for throughout the ages, regardless of colour, creed, religion, race, nationality, age, sex, wealth, ability or technological advancement.

People have taken a variety of different paths in trying to achieve inner peace: some through accumulating material possessions and wealth, others through drugs, some through music, others through meditation, some through their husbands and wives, others through their careers and some through their children's achievements. And the list goes on.

Yet the search also goes on. In our time we have been led to believe that technological advancement and modernisation will produce for us physical comforts and through these we will attain inner peace.

However, if we were to take the most technologically advanced and most industrialised nation in the world, America, then we would see that what we have been led to believe is not factual. The statistics show that in America some 20 million adults suffer from depression yearly; and what is depression but a total lack of inner peace? Furthermore in the year 2000 the death rate due to suicide was double the rate of those who die from Aids. However, the news media being what it is, we hear more about those who die from Aids than we do about those who die by committing suicide. Also, more people die from suicide in America than from homicide, and the homicide rates themselves are massive.

So the reality is that technological advancement and modernisation have not brought inner peace and tranquility. Rather, in spite of the creature comforts that modernisation has brought us, we are further away from inner peace than our ancestors were. Inner peace is for the most part of our lives very elusive; we never seem to get our hands on it.

Many of us mistake personal pleasures for inner peace; we achieve elements of pleasure from a variety of things, be it wealth, sexual relations or other than that. But these do not last, they come and go. Yes we have personal pleasures from time to time and we are pleased with various things from time to time, but this is not inner peace. True inner peace is a sense of stability and contentment which carries us through all the trials and difficulties of life.

We need to understand that peace is

not something that will exist in this world around us because when we define peace according to the dictionary definition, it states that peace is freedom from war or civil strife. Where do have this? There is always a war or some sort of civil unrest happening somewhere in the world. If we look at peace in terms of the state level, then peace is freedom from public disorder and security, but where in the world do we have this in a complete form? If we look at peace on a social level, family and work, then peace is freedom from disagreements and arguments, but is there such a social environment that never has disagreements or arguments? In terms of location, then yes, we can have a place which is calm, peaceful and tranquil, some islands for example, but this external peace only exists for a small amount of time, sooner or later a storm or a hurricane will come.

Allaah says:

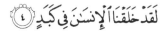

"Verily, I have created man in toil."

(Qur'aan 90: 4)

This is the nature of our lives; we are in toil and struggle, ups and downs, times of difficulties and times of ease. It is a life full of tests as Allaah says:

وَلَنَبْلُوَنَّكُم بِشَىْءٍ مِّنَ ٱلْخَوْفِ وَٱلْجُوعِ وَنَقْصٍ مِّنَ ٱلْأَمْوَٰلِ وَٱلْأَنفُسِ وَٱلثَّمَرَٰتِۗ وَبَشِّرِ ٱلصَّٰبِرِينَ ﴿١٥٥﴾

"And certainly, We shall test you with something of fear, hunger, loss of wealth, lives and fruits, but give glad tidings to the patient ones."

(Qur'aan: 2: 155)

To deal with our circumstances, the circumstances of toil and struggle in which we live, patience is the key. But if we go back to the inner peace that we are looking for, then patience cannot manifest itself if we do not have that inner peace. We are living in a world of toil and struggle, but yet within ourselves it is possible to attain inner peace — peace with the environment, with the world in which we live.

II

Obviously there are some obstacles which prevent us from attaining peace. First we have to identify the obstacles in our lives which prevent us from achieving maximum inner peace and develop some kind of strategy to remove them. The obstacles will not be removed just by thinking that we need to remove them; we have to develop some steps to achieve this. How do we go about removing these obstacles so that we can achieve what is possible of inner peace?

The first step is to identify the obstacles themselves. We have to be aware of them, because if we cannot identify them then we cannot remove them.

The second step is to accept them as obstacles within ourselves. For example, anger is one of the biggest obstacles to inner peace. If a person is angry, worked up and has blown a fuse, how can he or she have inner peace in that circumstance? It is not possible. So the person needs to recognize that anger is an obstacle to inner peace.

However, if a person states, "Yes, it is an obstacle but I do not get angry", then such a person has a problem. He has not accepted that obstacle as a problem and is in a state of self denial. As such he cannot remove it.

If we look at the obstacles in life we can put them under a variety of headings: personal problems, family issues, financial dilemmas, work pressures and spiritual confusion. And there are many issues under these headings.

We have so many problems and obstacles that they are like illnesses. If we try to deal with them one by one we will never get through them. We need to identify them, put them in some general categories and tackle them as a group as opposed to trying to tackle each individual obstacle and problem.

To do this we have to first of all remove obstacles that are beyond our control. We have to be able to distinguish which obstacles are within our control and which ones are beyond our control. While we perceive the ones that are beyond our control as obstacles, the reality is that they are not. They are the things that Allaah has destined for us in our lives. They are not really obstacles, but we have misinterpreted them as being obstacles.

For example, in this time one might find oneself born black in a world that favours white people over black people; or born poor in a world that favours the rich over the poor, or born short, or crippled, or any other physical condition which is considered a handicap.

These are all things that were and are beyond our control. We did not choose which family to be born into; we did not choose which body for our spirit to be blown into — this is not our choice. So whatever we find of these kinds of obstacles, we just have to be patient with them and realize that, in fact, they are not really obstacles. Allaah told us:

كُتِبَ عَلَيۡكُمُ ٱلۡقِتَالُ وَهُوَ كُرۡهٌ لَّكُمۡ وَعَسَىٰٓ أَن تَكۡرَهُواْ شَيۡـًٔا وَهُوَ خَيۡرٌ لَّكُمۡ وَعَسَىٰٓ أَن تُحِبُّواْ شَيۡـًٔا وَهُوَ شَرٌّ لَّكُمۡ وَٱللَّهُ يَعۡلَمُ وَأَنتُمۡ لَا تَعۡلَمُونَ ﴿٢١٦﴾

"…and it may be that you dislike a thing which is good for you and that

you like a thing which is bad for you.
Allaah knows but you do not know."

(Qur'aan: 2: 216)

So the obstacles that are beyond our
control, we may dislike them and we
may want to change them, and some
people actually spend a lot of money
trying to change them. Michael Jackson
is a classic example. He was born black
in a world that favours white people, so
he spent a lot of money trying to change
himself but he only ended up making a
mess of himself.

Inner peace can only be achieved if
the obstacles that are beyond our control

are accepted by us patiently as part of Allaah's destiny. Know that whatever happens which we had or have no control over, then Allaah has put in it some good, whether or not we are able to grasp what is good in it; the good is still there. So we accept it!

III

There was an article in a newspaper which had a photograph of a smiling Egyptian man. He had a smile on his face from ear to ear with his hands stretched out and both thumbs sticking up; his father was kissing him on one cheek and his sister on the other cheek. Underneath the photograph it had a caption. He was supposed to have been on a Gulf Air flight the day before from Cairo to Bahrain. He had dashed down to the airport to catch the flight and when he got there, he had one stamp missing on his passport. In Cairo you have to have many stamps on your documents. You get this person to stamp this and sign that and that person to stamp that and sign this. But there he was at the airport with one stamp missing. As he was a teacher in Bahrain and this flight was the last one back to Bahrain which would enable him to report back on time, missing it meant that he would have lost his job. So he nagged them to let him on the flight. He became frantic, started crying and screaming and going berserk, but he could not get on the plane. It took off without him. He went to his home in Cairo distraught, thinking that he was finished and that his career was over. His family comforted him and told him not to worry about it. The next day, he heard the news that the plane he was meant to be on crashed and everybody on board died. And then there he was, ecstatic that he did not make the flight. But the day before, it seemed the end of his life, a tragedy that he did not get on the flight.

These are signs, and such signs can be found in the story of Moosa and Khidr (peace be upon them) in Soorah al-Kahf which we should read every Friday. When Khidr made a hole in the boat of the people who were kind enough to take him and Moosa across the river, Moosa asked why he did that. When the owners of the boat saw the hole in the boat they wondered who did it and thought that it was a nasty thing to have done. A short while later the king came down to the river and forcefully took away all the boats except the one with a hole in it. So the owners of the boat praised Allaah due to the fact that there was a hole in their boat.

There are other obstacles or rather things which are perceived as obstacles in our life. These are things in which we cannot figure out what is beyond them. A thing happens and we do not know why — we do not have an explanation for it. For some people, this drives them into disbelief. If one listens to an atheist, he has no inner peace and has rejected God. Why did that person become an atheist? It is abnormal to disbelieve in

God, whereas it is normal for us to believe in God because Allaah created us with a natural inclination to believe in Him. The Prophet Muhammad (*sallallaahu alaihi wa sallam* — may peace and blessings be upon him) said:

"Every child is born with a pure nature — as a Muslim, with a natural inclination to believe in God…"

This is the nature of human beings, but a person who becomes an atheist without having been taught it from childhood usually does so because of a tragedy. If a tragedy happens in their life they have no explanations as to why it happened.

For example, a person who became an atheist may say that he or she had a wonderful auntie; she was a very good person and everybody loved her, but one day whilst she was out crossing the road a car came out of nowhere and hit her and she died. Why did this happen to her of all people? Why? No explanations! Or a person who became an atheist may have had a child who died and say: why did this happen to my child? Why? No explanations! As a result of such tragedies they then think that there can't possibly be a God.

THE SEARCH FOR INNER PEACE

Going back to the story of Moosa and Khidr, after they crossed the river they came across a child and Khidr cut that child's head off. Moosa asked Khidr how he could possibly do such a thing? The child was innocent and Khidr cut his head off! Khidr told Moosa that the child had righteous parents and if the child had grown up, Allaah knew that he would have become such a terror for his parents that he would have driven them into disbelief, so Allaah ordered the death of the child. Of course, the parents grieved when they found their child dead. However, Allaah replaced their child with one who was righteous and better for them. This child honoured them and was good to and for them, but the parents would always have a hole in their heart due to losing their first child, right until the Day of Judgement when they will stand before Allah and He will reveal to them the reason why He took the soul of their first child and then they will then understand and praise Allaah.

So this is the nature of our lives. There are things, things which are apparently negative, things which happen in our lives which seem to be obstacles to inner peace because we do not understand them or why they happened to us, but we have to put them aside. They are from Allaah and we have to believe that ultimately there is good behind them, whether we can see it or not. Then we move on to those things that we can change. First we identify them, then we move to the second major step and that is removing the obstacles by developing solutions for them. To remove the obstacles we have to focus mostly on self-change and this is because Allaah says:

$$\text{لَهُۥ مُعَقِّبَٰتٌ مِّنۢ بَيۡنِ يَدَيۡهِ وَمِنۡ خَلۡفِهِۦ يَحۡفَظُونَهُۥ مِنۡ أَمۡرِ ٱللَّهِۗ إِنَّ ٱللَّهَ لَا يُغَيِّرُ مَا بِقَوۡمٍ حَتَّىٰ يُغَيِّرُواْ مَا بِأَنفُسِهِمۡۗ وَإِذَآ أَرَادَ ٱللَّهُ بِقَوۡمٍ سُوٓءًا فَلَا مَرَدَّ لَهُۥۚ وَمَا لَهُم مِّن دُونِهِۦ مِن وَالٍ ۝}$$

"Verily, Allaah will not change the good condition of a people as long as they do not change their state of good within themselves..."

(Qur'aan: 13: 11)

This is an area which we have control over. We can even develop patience, although the common idea is that some people are just born patient. A man came to the Prophet (peace be upon him) and asked what he needed to do to get to paradise, so the Prophet told him:

"Do not get angry."

The man was an individual who would get angry quickly, so the Prophet told the man that he needed to do change his angry nature. So changing oneself and one's character is something achievable. The Prophet (peace be upon him) also said:

"Whoever pretends to be patient, with a desire to be patient, Allaah will give him patience."

This means that although some people are born patient the rest of us can learn to be patient.

Interestingly in Western psychiatry and psychology they used to tell us to get it off our chest, don't hold it in because if we did we would explode, so better to let it all out. Later on they discovered that when people let it all out small blood vessels would burst in their brain because they were so angry. They found that it was actually dangerous and potentially damaging to let it all out. So now they say it is better not to let it all out.

The Prophet told us to try to be patient, so externally we should give that façade of being patient even when internally we are boiling. And we do not try to be patient externally in order to deceive people; rather, we do so in order to develop patience. If we are consistent in this then the external image of patience also becomes internal and as a result, complete patience is achieved and is achievable as mentioned in the hadeeth quoted above.

IV

Among the methods is to look at how the material elements of our lives play a major part with regards to patience and us achieving it. The Prophet (peace be upon him) gave us advice on how to deal with these elements by saying:

"Do not look to those above you who are more fortunate, instead, look to those below you or less fortunate..."

This is because no matter what our situation is, there are always those who are worse off than us. This should be our general strategy with regards to the material life. Nowadays the material life is a huge part of our life, we seem to be obsessed with it; gaining all we can in this world seems to be the main point that most of us focus our energies towards. So if one must do this, then they should not let it affect their inner peace. While dealing with the material world we should not keep focusing on those who are better off than us otherwise we will never be satisfied with what we have. The Prophet (peace be upon him) said:

"If you give the son of Adam a valley of gold, he would want another one."

They say that the grass is always greener on the other side; the more a person has, the more a person wants. We cannot achieve satisfaction in the material world if we are chasing after it in such a way; rather, we should look to those who are less fortunate, this way we will remember the gifts, benefits and mercy that Allaah has bestowed upon us with regards to our own wealth, no matter how little it may seem.

There is another hadeeth which helps us in the realm of the material world to put our affairs in their proper perspective, and is a Prophetic example of Steven Covey's principle of "first things first". The Prophet (peace be upon him) stated this principle over one thousand, four hundred years ago and laid this principle down for the believers by saying,

"Whoever makes this world his goal Allaah will confuse his affairs and place poverty before his eyes and he will be able to attain nothing from this world except for what Allaah has already written for him..."

So a person's affairs will not come together for him, he will be all over the place, like a chicken with its head cut off, running wild if he makes this world his goal. Allaah will place poverty before his eyes and no matter how much money he has he will feel poor. Every time someone is nice to him or smiles at him he feels that they are only doing so because they want his money, he can't trust anyone and is not happy.

When the stock market crashes you read about some of those who invested in it committing suicide. A person may have had eight million and lost five million with three million left after the market crashed, but losing that five million seems to him to be the end. He sees no point in living after that, as Allaah has put poverty between his eyes.

We have to keep in mind that a person will not get from this world except what Allaah has already written for them, this is the bottom line. After all that running around, staying up late at night, being a workaholic a person will only get that which Allaah has already destined for him or her. The Prophet (peace be upon him) said:

"Whoever sets the hereafter as his goal, Allaah gathers his affairs for him, gives him richness of faith in the heart and the world will come to him grudgingly and submissively."

Such a person attains richness of the heart. Richness is not about having a lot of wealth, but richness is having wealth of the heart, and what is wealth of the heart? It is contentment, and this is where the peace comes from, when a person submits themselves to Allaah, and this is Islam.

The inner peace is accepting Islam in our hearts and living by the principles of Islam. So Allaah will put richness in a person's heart and this world will come to him submissively, on its knees and humbled. Such a person will not have to chase it. This is the promise of the Prophet if a person puts "first things first", and that is the hereafter. If it is paradise that we want, then that should be manifest in our lives. It should be the point of our focus — what we keep putting in the forefront.

V

So how do we know when the hereafter is our focus? If we sit down with a person and all we talk about are the latest cars, expensive houses, travelling, holidays and money, if the majority of our conversations is about material things or it is gossip, talking about this person and that person then it means that the hereafter is not our focus. If the hereafter was our focus then it would be reflected in our conversation. This is a very basic level in which we can judge ourselves, so we should stop and ask ourselves, "what do we spend most of our time talking about"? If we find that our priority is this world, then we need to re-focus, we need to put "first things first", meaning the hereafter before the life of this world, and if we do this we can achieve inner peace, and Allaah informed us of this in the Qur'aan, a precise step to take in order to attain inner peace, and Allaah says:

ٱلَّذِينَ ءَامَنُوا۟ وَتَطْمَئِنُّ قُلُوبُهُم بِذِكْرِ ٱللَّهِ أَلَا بِذِكْرِ ٱللَّهِ تَطْمَئِنُّ ٱلْقُلُوبُ ﴿٢٨﴾

"Verily, in the remembrance of Allaah do hearts find rest."

(Qur'aan: 13: 28)

So it is only by the remembrance of Allaah that hearts find rest. This is the inner peace. The remembrance of Allaah is in everything we do as Muslims. Islam is living a life remembering Allaah, and Allaah says:

إِنَّنِى أَنَا ٱللَّهُ لَا إِلَٰهَ إِلَّا أَنَا۠ فَٱعْبُدْنِى وَأَقِمِ ٱلصَّلَوٰةَ لِذِكْرِىٓ ﴿١٤﴾

"Perform the prayer for my remembrance…"

(Qur'aan: 20: 14)

As Muslims, everything that we do involves the remembrance of Allaah. Allaah says:

قُلْ إِنَّ صَلَاتِي وَنُسُكِي وَمَحْيَاىَ وَمَمَاتِي لِلَّهِ رَبِّ ٱلْعَٰلَمِينَ ۝

"Say: Indeed, my prayer, my sacrifice, my living and dying are for Allaah, Lord of all the worlds."

(Qur'aan: 6: 162)

So here is the way to achieve inner peace: to remember Allaah in all aspects of our lives. This remembrance or dhikr is not as some people think; that is, to sit in the corner of a dark room constantly repeating "Allaah, Allaah, Allaah…" This is not how we remember Allaah. Yes, such a person is saying Allaah's name, but if we think about it, if somebody came to you and for example your name is Muhammad and kept saying "Muhammad, Muhammad, Muhammad…" you would wonder what is wrong with that person. Does he want something? Is there something that he needs? What is the purpose of repeating my name without further talk?

This is not the way to remember Allaah because this is not how the Prophet (peace be upon him) remembered Allaah and there is no record of him doing that. Some people say that we should remember Allaah by dancing around or swaying from side to side. This is not the way to remember Allaah, as this too is not how the Prophet remembered Allaah and there is no record of him doing that.

The Prophet (peace be upon him) remembered Allaah in his life. His life was a life of remembrance of Allaah. He lived a life in remembrance of Allaah and this is the true remembrance: in our prayers and in our living and our dying.

VI

In summary, the search for inner peace involves recognizing the problems that we have in our lives, recognizing our obstacles, recognizing that inner peace will only come when we identify those obstacles and understand which of them we can change and that we focus on those obstacles we can change — the ones which are related to our self. If we change our self, then Allaah will change the world around us and give us the means to deal with the world around us. Even though the world is in turmoil, Allaah gives us inner peace with it.

Whatever happens we know that it is Allaah's destiny and that it is Allaah's trials. We know that ultimately it is for our good and has good in it. Allaah created this world, and us in it, as a means to attain paradise. The trials of this world are for our own spiritual growth. If we can accept all this, accepting Allaah in our hearts, then we can find inner peace.

ABOUT THE AUTHOR

Dr. Bilal Philips is a Jamaican Canadian Islamic Scholar who accepted Islam after journeying politically and intellectually from Christianity to Communism. His desire to seek in-depth knowledge has taken him to Madinah, Riyadh and the UK, where he completed his BA, MA and PhD in Islamic Theology.

Considered one of the most influential Islamic scholars today, he is the founder and chancellor of International Open University with over half a million students from 250 countries.

CPSIA information can be obtained
at www.ICGtesting.com
Printed in the USA
LVHW030218080922
727800LV00004B/406